Modern Fairy Tales

Modern Fairy Tales

poetry | art | words

K. Towne Jr.

CICO BOOKS
LONDON NEW YORK

Published in 2018 by CICO Books
An imprint of Ryland Peters & Small Ltd
20–21 Jockey's Fields   341 E 116th St
London WC1R 4BW   New York, NY 10029

www.rylandpeters.com

10 9 8 7 6 5 4 3 2 1

A CIP catalog record for this book is available from the
Library of Congress and the British Library.

ISBN: 978-1-78249-664-9

Printed in China

Cover design concept: Phebe de Guzman
Illustrator: Amy Louise Evans

Commissioning editor: Kristine Pidkameny
Senior editor: Carmel Edmonds
Junior designer: Eliana Holder
Art director: Sally Powell
Production controller: Mai-Ling Collyer
Publishing manager: Penny Craig
Publisher: Cindy Richards

Contents

Introduction

Like so many things in this world, my passion for writing has ebbed and flowed. While I dabbled in poetry as a form of expression in my teens, it wasn't until my mid 20s that I found a purpose for my writing. As I started to pay more and more attention to the world around I me, I saw how beautiful its people and places could be. But, with age comes wisdom, and I was overwhelmed by how much unnecessary ugly existed as well. So, frustrated with this ratio, it became my focus to affect this balance to the best of my ability. If one line, one poem, or one word could make just one person's life better in any way, then why not write it? If you can share any experience, and have even one person relate to it, benefit from what you've learned, or simply enjoy the moment with you, then why would you ever keep it to yourself?

I don't want to mislead you. Not every piece in this book will make you happy. In fact, I can guarantee you that many of them are rooted quite deeply in pain. What I think is important to remember is that things don't have to be inherently happy or positive to be beautiful. A broken heart is one of the worst of mankind's creations, yet it is also a reminder of our ability to love, and to heal.

With this thought, I give to you my first book. A collection built over years. Love, loss, pain, and wonder all make their appearances in these pages. So, if you can find one poem, one piece, or a single line that makes your life better, makes you think, or simply makes you smile, then I promise you, all of this has been worth it.

To Kaitlyn, for helping me find my pen again.

To Christina, for reminding me what it feels like to fall in love.

To Madison, for showing me how to turn sunsets into skylines.

To Katelyn, my Alice, for turning every brick wall into a rabbit hole.

To Stephanie, my person, for showing me the best things in life are worth waiting for.

And to you, of course, for everything in between.

You know those few magic moments,
when your eyes first open for the day?

That magic space between fantasy and reality,
where your mind can never stay.

That feeling you get when you're so deep in
a book that the world around you fades.

That exact moment the sun rises, and turns
darkness into day.

The first moment you realize you're in love,
and are at a loss for what to say,
I hope that's where I find you,
and for the brief moments you're in these pages,
I hope that that's where you stay.

If the last day I spent on this earth,
I got to kiss you goodnight,
that would be enough.

enough

"You never wrote me my poem," she said to me,
somewhere between anger and sadness.

Silly girl, I thought. My pen had been left
untouched for years, and it wasn't until her
that I picked it up again. So, as I thumbed
through the dozens of things I had written, I
looked at her and said,

*"Just because something doesn't have your name
on it, doesn't mean it isn't yours."*

She looked at me confused, but I know someday
she'll understand.

                                    beginnings

These words are my poison, this whiskey my savior,
but the only habit I admit to is this pen and her paper.
I'm afraid of success, and best friends with the fall,
and if that sounds backwards to you, then you don't
know me at all.

So, drink up this ink, pour stories into your glass
Keep your dreams alive, or become resigned to the past.
Chasing immortality in ink, clinging desperately to life.
Funny how the thought of death makes one want to
write.

So, remember my words, this is the favor I ask;
For the body is temporary, art is what lasts.

heaven & horcruxes

Sometimes

a heart must be broken

to slip through the bars

of its cage

escape

Miss me with all your heart,
or darling,
don't miss me at all.
Love was never meant to be
measured in maybe's
or
I think so's.

in or out

My heart is too big to hold everyone in it,
so I often leave people and places behind.
I live too in the moment to dwell on the past,
discarding memories along the way.
I used to hold my grudges,
always searching for something to blame for my
own faults.
When I was younger I used to think I escaped,
but now, I realize all I did was leave.
You may mark my absence as intentionally malicious,
but, if anything, it's unintentionally indifferent.
I have no problem picking it back up in the moment,
because that's the beauty of no hard feelings,
there's nothing to turn off.

I can commit as much as any function or
weekend demands,
and would hardly call it a chore.
But then I'll be gone.
I would apologize,
but what would I be apologizing for?

childhood

The world today rejects the chase,
and I think it's the tragedy of our time.
Triple text. Chase them down.
Embarrass yourself.
EARN it,
and for god's sake,
try.
Everyone is too scared
to look like a fool,
but a cool demeanor
can lead to a cold heart.
Stop chasing for too long,
and you just might forget how,
and in a game of Hide and Hide,
I promise there are no winners.

modern bravery

I find comfort in thunderstorms,
and I think it's because
in those brief moments,
the world outside my window
matches the madness inside my head.

thoughts & thunder

Sunsets and short breaths,
Happy endings and untimely deaths.

We were, in a way, our very own fairy tale.
Dragons and princesses, in form of baggage
and beautiful voices.
Underlying morals, poorly hidden in tearful
and impossible choices.

Ever after never showed,
but that's typically ever after's thing.
Chasing a future,
only to catch it,
pin it down,
and demand that you leave it be.

We were, in a way, our very own fairy tale,
yet this is the part where I leave you be.
But if you ever believe in fairy tales again,
you know where you can find me.

waiting...

So what if heartbreaks have
left their mark upon you?
You shouldn't want it any
other way,
for without brushstrokes,
we are but blank canvas.

You wouldn't snuff out a candle
then be disappointed when there is no flame,
so, I ask you all, for the love of god,
why can't we treat people just the same?

the destruction of our youth

If fairy tales
have taught us anything,
It's that we fall in love
with short stories
the most

I visited a used bookstore today.
I think I was trying to forget you.

Trying to get lost in someone else's story, but
still stuck on all the things you've said.
I must have flipped through 100 books before I
realized I couldn't get you off my mind,

because with thousands of stories of love and loss
surrounding me,
it was no different than what was going on
inside my head.

paperback scents & similar sorrows

If you want to learn to love,
let Mother Nature be your guide.

The way her fire dances with any partner in
its path.

The way her rain falls to the earth,
hard and strong and fast.

The way ocean waves tirelessly massage the shore.

How night and day lose to each other,
but never keep a score.

How the trees can shed their leaves,
accepting every death.

How a fire can clear a forest,
and new life grows by what it left.

How her wind can fill our sails,
while she asks for nothing in return.

For when you understand how Mother Nature loves,
you'll find humans have much to learn.

mother knows best

A city at night is a wonderful sight,
but what of one light in a storm?
The cold gaze of millions
means damn next to nothing,
compared to a home that is warm.

home

Lying in the middle of the street at 1am,
our little act of rebellion against a world
stacked so heavily against us,
we held hands as we watched the stars
literally fall from the sky,
feeling that maybe, just in that moment,
they were doing so just for us.
So, as we lay there, trying to figure out
why any of us were on this earth in the
first place,
I looked at her, and the answer came,
beautiful and easy.
This.
This is why.

rebels

To *intertwine* your happiness with someone else's is something so *dangerously brave, so inherently idiotic,* but so *incomprehensibly, undeniably human.*

worth it

Calm her chaos,
but never silence
her storm

A dead rose sits atop my
dresser, and somehow, I'm
reminded of you and me.
Beautiful at first,
poetically sad at the end,
an artifact of a memory that
can never be perfect again.
Like my love for you,
I still have it to this day,
But as the time carries on,
I can do nothing but watch,
as it withers away.

withered

My love for you is Peter Pan,
endlessly playful in Neverland.
It is Snow White, saved by a kiss,
as only true love's kiss ever can.
It is Harry Potter, in the forbidden forest,
walking selflessly to his death.
It follows you, like Hansel and Gretel, chasing
every crumb you've left.
It is the Brothers Grimm, protecting you from
every demon that's been caught.
It is Mulan, marching on, stronger for every
battle that's been fought.
It is all these, and so much more; every fairy
tale is based on you;
for as you sleep, within my arms,
I realize,
fairy tales do come true.

                                        ever after

Like the leaves to the earth,
there was beauty in the way
I fell for you.

lost with **you**,

in **you**,

and without **you**

Am I a *loner?*
Or just *lonely?*
...

Get caught in the rain.

Hike during a storm.

Camp in your backyard if you have to,
but make this world your own.

We all crave sunny days for the beach and cool
breezes in the mountains,
but I challenge you to want more.

Hike in the desert in high heat.

Spend a cold night in a dark forest.

Do everything you think is backwards because
there's so much beauty to be had on the other
side of easy.

That's not to say there isn't beauty to the
beach in summer,
but have you ever been at sea while it rains?

Embrace the storm, welcome the
heat, and go dancing in the
rain!

And when you fall in
love, my friend, I ask
you to do the same.

challenge everything

The universe is a strange place.
Stardust falls at random,
and humans fall in love.

cosmic rain

Young, with skyline dreams.
Dressed up in a city that dressed down dreams.
A heart full of love, and a head full of steam,
99 pounds of confidence,
and not an ounce of self-esteem.

Her eyes will beg you to love her,
yet her mouth won't say a word.
She accepts her fate as punishment,
for some unknown debt she has incurred.

So, as your eyes travel down her dress
And back up again with pleasure,
Know that it's not in her frame, but her frame
of mind,
That you truly find the treasure.

Cigarettes, and deep regrets
For certain choices that she's made.
I mean—rent's expensive, so her mind's a mess,
She wasn't raised to be a maid.

I'm running out of space it seems,
to describe her as she deserves,
just know that if you sat down at her table,
you'd be lucky to get served hors d'oeuvres.

skyline dreams

That's the thing about my dream girls:
one of us always wakes up.

The best part about
the world is that it
allows you to wear
different faces.

The worst part is
that it demands it.

                    masks

There is no shame
in abandoning a sinking ship,
but only the weak
jump at the first sign
of a storm

Her eyes were fire, mesmerizing and warm.
Life-giving and dangerous.
A reminder of an ancient power,
both friend and foe,
that protected while refusing to be tamed.

Her lips were the ocean, soft and salty sweet.
Powerful and ever changing.
A single taste reminded you of home,
of love,
of loss.
Of all the childhood dreams you've forgotten,
Of unmanifested fears conquered before
their prime.

Her laughter was rain, beautiful and soft.
Millions of tiny pieces that muffled the world
when whole.
Soaked to the bone, and there was only her.

She. The sun and the storm.
The sea and the shore.
She laughed,
and the rain poured down around me.

soaking wet

Endless clouds, atop rolling hills, ablaze in autumn's splendor.

A lesson hidden in the beauty of nature's pastel surrender.

Leaves fear not change, nor storm, nor even death; they simply live to be.

How unobtainable it is, for mankind to understand this kind of bravery.

The bravery to meet with death, without resistance, and without sorrow;

a calm and unwavering confidence, in the promise of tomorrow.

A humbling tale, of what transpires, deep within our natural laws.

For while humans live with the fear of death, the leaves dance as they fall.

Such a sight, and what a wonder, to witness such a calming act.

If only humanity had it within them to have such poise and tact.

So, as you watch, I hope you learn, that struggle is not the only way.

Live your life the way you desire, and let the end come as it may.

leaf lessons

My heart won't give me answers,
but at least this whiskey tries.
A fire rages in my gut,
replacing long dead butterflies.

I'm not sure what I'm running towards,
but I know what I'm running from.
So easy to drown yourself in darkness,
when you thought she was the one.

So, I search for answers in a bottle
(I mean, it never hurts to look)
but deep down I know I'll never find
that piece of me she took.

forged in flame

I think of her sometimes, afterwards.
I'm not proud of it,
but it's true.
Lying naked next to you in bed,
my body satisfied but my mind restless,
she inhabits more rooms in my mind than I'd
like to admit.
I've never pretended you were her though.
I'm not that cruel.
For the absolute nothing that that's worth,
it's true.

                              worthless

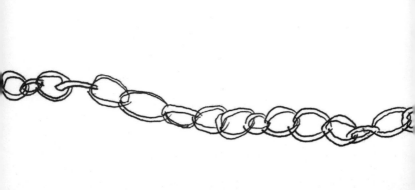

I was upset that I was paying for sins I
didn't commit,
but I never stopped to realize that you
were the one in prison.

So funny how I thought I saved you from all
this shit,
when we both know it was never my decision.

But I like to think I played my part,
and hopefully played it well,
and I think someday that you'll agree
but I suppose only time shall tell.

                    you saved me too

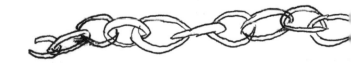

Home

is where the heart is,

and I've never felt so

homeless.

It's funny to me how people describe
heartbreak as a singular thing, a moment,
when I find it to be quite the opposite.
Sure, I cried that night, but that's not
what heartbreak is to me. It's every time
I see her, and being forced to accept that
she's no longer mine. It's coming across
something beautiful, and wishing she was
there to see it. It's talking about my dream
vacation, and realizing I'm imagining her
there with me. It's staring wistfully at the
cherry in my Manhattan, because I know
she would've stolen it if she were here. So,
while my heart *broke* the moment I lost
her, heartbreak isn't about how I miss her,
it's feeling everything she's missing from.
Heartbreak is a lot of things, but
over never seems to be one.

tu me manques

Whiskey cokes and fairy tales
have one thing in common.

I believe in both.

religion

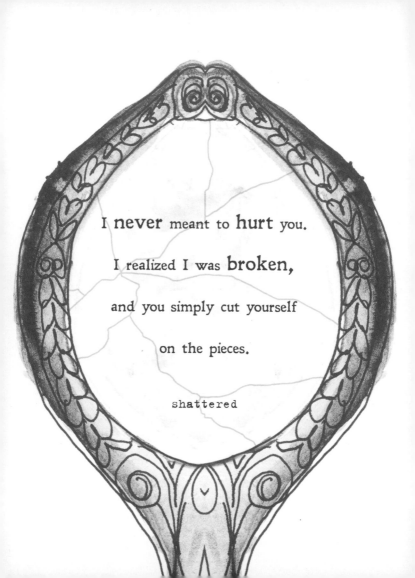

I never meant to hurt you.

I realized I was broken,

and you simply cut yourself

on the pieces.

shattered

Falling for you was like falling down the stairs.
I was in complete control, then, without warning,
I was spinning, tumbling, and I had no idea why or how.
Then, before I even knew what had happened,
I lay at the bottom; shocked, stunned,
and so oddly aware that I still ended up exactly
where I was trying to go.

falling in flight

I want to grab life by the throat and rip the mask off of reality.

I want to jump off of a building and fly to prove I don't respect gravity.

I want to flip everything I know upside down just to change my perspective.

I want to do everything you tell me backwards to prove I answer to no objective.

Because here's the thing:

No one owns you.

Not in theory, not for salary, or because of debt.

So, if you think you can do better, I'm willing to take that bet.

I believe in every human who thinks they have a chance,

and I respect any soul that's brave enough to dance.

Because here's the thing:

No one owns you.

We are so much more than they try to make us all believe,

trying to keep us down because they're afraid of how well we'll lead.

So, answer to no one, live only by your own rules and religion,

because whether they all like it not, freedom is a human condition.

freedom

We never want what we have,
craving only what we've lost
Obsessed with our redemption,
no matter what the cost
Consumed by our losses, we are
haunted in our sleep.
And we, too foolish to realize,
it is but ghosts we seek.

phantoms

We all drink poison known as
someone else's plan for our reality,
and then we wonder why the
world is sick.

corporate kool-aid

love me softly,

slowly,

and wholly

or don't love me at all

Don't be so quick to
judge someone's path,
lest you forget where
your own started,
or before too long,
you'll be too far gone,
and you'll fail to
appreciate how and why
they parted.

humbled crossings

Someone's killed my mind!
Oh no,
what have they done?
  But when I look down at
  my hand,
      I realize I'm holding
      the gun.
      Oh.

                    help

How is it that you fit so perfectly in my arms, but so impossibly into my life?

beautiful conundrum

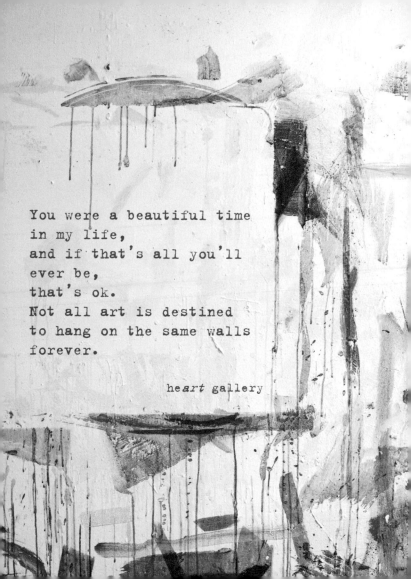

You were a beautiful time
in my life,
and if that's all you'll
ever be,
that's ok.
Not all art is destined
to hang on the same walls
forever.

heart gallery

Our love was fierce and reckless, far too wild to be tamed,

so, while we couldn't make it last,

I love you for it all the same

manhattans

I've never met God to see his eyes,

but I've met the Devil,
and her eyes are green.

blu

My mind wanders, as do I,
across endless oceans and sunset skies,
leaving pieces of my soul in distant places,
giving pieces of my heart to different faces.

I chase my dreams around the globe,
a better person for every sight I see,
wishing I could leave my mark on the world,
as easily as it leaves its mark on me.

wanderlust scars

Man is so brave that he can
glimpse the most distant light
in our universe,

yet so timid,
that he's afraid to see the light within his own heart.

insignificance

Don't try too hard to fall in *love* with people.
Fall in *love* with the world, and I promise,
it will fall in *love* right back.

true soulmates

You said "us"
—and in that moment,
I knew words
were magic.

I've made a lot of mistakes in my life,
but if every single one had to happen
to make sure that I was right here,
right now,
to meet you,
then I forgive myself for them all.

every. single. one.

Some girls are made of sugar and spice
and everything nice,
But not her.
She's made of stardust and wanderlust,
and has tried to kill me more than twice.
And honestly,
I can't think of anything sexier.

shark attacks and kitten claws

I'm not afraid of falling in *love*.
I'm afraid of being the only one who does,
the only one who *loves*.

Afraid that when I play tug of war with
heartstrings,
I'll be the only one who tugs.

muddy

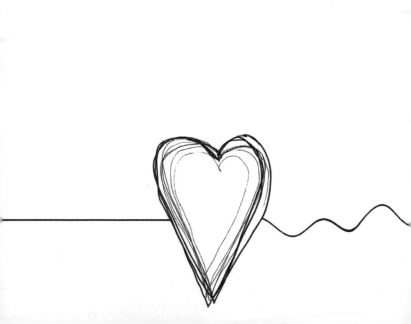

You make me want to write,
or cry
or fight,
or die,
but of all the things you make
me want to do,
loving you
is the hardest

fighting

Love her or leave her,
The choice will keep you sane,
but I envy not the man
for which they are one and the same.

impossible

She was my hurricane. My storm.
My conquest and my fears.
But then there was *her*.
My calm sea, my island breeze,
my paradise.

They say that calm seas never
made a good sailor,
and deep down I'm afraid they
don't make a good lover.

i'm sorry.

sunken

My mind felt beautiful yesterday,
alone amongst the snow-laden trees.
The cold strong enough to bite my face,
but proud of my ability to fight it.
There's something to be said
for leaving a single set of footprints
on a white, untouched canvas.
The silence a beautiful conversation.
Here I am at work today,
unable to notice any real sign of my existence
against the white, unforgiving light.
These headphones cancel out the noise,
but nothing can drown out this reality.
Such an impractical thing to wish,
that snow could fall in cubicles.
But, then again, I suppose
we all have different
ideas about what's
impractical.

impractical

When I look for *perfect*,
perfect is all I see,
because when I look for *perfect*,
it's you staring back at me.

you

I'm in love!
Do you hear me?
I'm in love!
Stupidly, recklessly, and
overwhelmingly in love.

You're probably looking for a poem,
but honestly, I don't have one.
That's not really my fault though.
I mean, I'm in love, goddamn it!
I've been a little busy.

distracted

Of all the music I've ever heard,

it's your voice that calms my soul.

Our lives may not
have fit together,
but ohhh did our souls know
how to dance...

She's beautiful.

Her face, of course! But I meant the way she
smiles at every homeless person we pass.
Her body, oh my god! But I meant the way she
laughs.

She's beautiful.

The way she's always there.
The way she walks, like she knows exactly
what she's worth.
The way she believes in people's dreams.

Do you hear me?

You're beautiful.

the details

You never lost me.

I lost myself before we ever met.

timeline

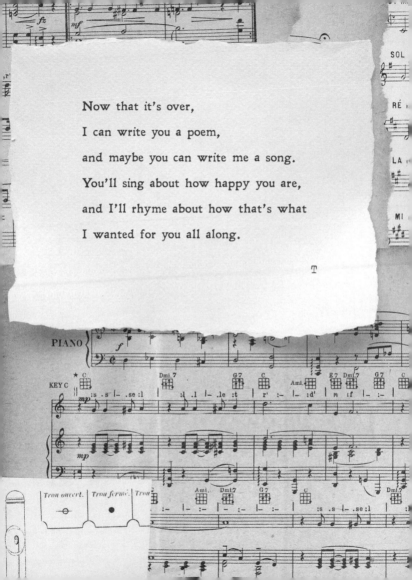

Now that it's over,

I can write you a poem,

and maybe you can write me a song.

You'll sing about how happy you are,

and I'll rhyme about how that's what

I wanted for you all along.

I want so hard to make you understand,
that it's not a game we're playing.
Not with the level we are at,
nor with the things that we've been saying.
Game or not, I'm scared to lose,
and terrified there is no winning,
Even with all the times we've laughed,
or the pleasure from our nights of sinning.

I want so hard to be your hero,
and I think I've put on a valiant show,
but this battle has left its mark on me,
I'm not sure how much farther I can go.
I've made my moves, and risked it big,
so maybe this was all a game,
but even if I've had my turn,
I think you've used me just the same.

So easy to see, once you're off the board,
the part you were meant to play.
But there is no tougher truth than the one learned
in youth, that you can't always get your way.
So, to summarize everything I've learned into a
single thesis,

*"To the Queen, in a game of chess, even the Knights
are just mere pieces."*

blu moon

I saw two girls dancing by jazz light tonight,
illuminated by the sound of the archway.

Their bodies kept time with the rhythm,
but their hearts fluttered to the beat of each other.

Cupid had spoken, and with all of his training,
it's not as if one would expect a stutter.

The moon played casually across faces that were
anything but,
and I thought,
"How beautiful it is to see the sky merge with
the ocean,
when it so often crashes on the shore."

                                        jazzlight

Reality is what you make it.

Your mind is only a prison if you
imagine it with bars.

make-believe keys

Why is it that when I'm drunk and in love,
no one believes me?

Yet the earth is always spinning,
and no one questions its intentions.

faithless

I hang my dreams neatly, on space-saving hangers,
tucked quietly between well-pressed suits.
I leave them there so that they feel dressed up
and important,
even though I never take them anywhere nice.
When I'm alone, at night, I let them out to play.
But only for a moment—they know the rules,
and in my room they stay.
They're not made for this world, or so they've
been told,
so, when my alarm goes off, it's back on the
hangers for them.
I apologize every day, as I pick out something
else to wear,
and in their wonder, in their brilliance, they
forgive me every time.
I do not deserve them, as they do not deserve
their fate.
Lost among worthless outfits and muttered apologies
about how I'm running late.

big dreams & small closets

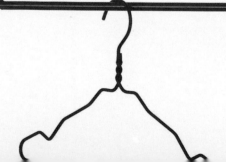

"Tell me you love me," she said.

Why? I've told her so many times, why does
she need to hear it again? But then, I
thought, maybe it's different every time.
Every *"I love you"* is the entire collection
of your experiences, both together, and as
individuals. Every heartbreak, tear, every
smile and laugh. It's not repetitive, because
you've never heard this *"I love you"* before
and, after your next smile, you
never can again.

"I love you," I said, this
epiphany spreading slowly
across my face. All she
did was smile, as if to
say she had known this
all already, and maybe,
just maybe, that was why
she asked.

1 4 3 x ∞

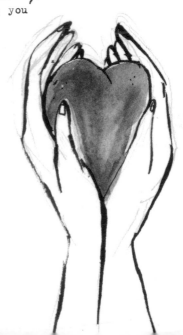

If scars are permanent then so are people.
We never really lose anyone.

for better or for worse

I don't need your fandom,
nor do I require your affirmation.
I don't do this for you.
Not entirely.
That's not to say that I don't want you to
get lost in these lines.
To feel it,
and maybe, deep down,
to even call it
art.
That's not to say I don't want my words to
touch you,
but if you don't like the way they feel as
they lay against your skin,
that's fine.
I learned long ago the difference between
want and need,
and you, my friend,
would be wise to do the same.

                    the doom of desire

The earth is nothing
but a rock,
careening recklessly
through space,
so with all the magic
in that kind of
randomness,
why would you ever feel
out of place?

you belong

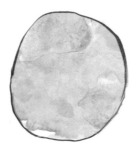

You're all so busy
trying to be tough,
that you've forgotten
how to be brave,
for if you never let
yourself become lost,
you'll never know what
it is to be saved.

modern martyr

Have you ever seen a girl so beautiful?
I swear the only reason the sun rises is
because the world wants to show her off.

reason enough

You're afraid your chaos will leave you lonely,
but love comes in many forms,
so while some people prefer sunsets,
so many fall for storms.

rage on

I've had my fair share of heartbreak,
But baby,
They don't make whiskey
Strong enough for you

bulleit proof

She was simple, not in the mind,
but in the way she was to be understood.
An intricate puzzle;
forming a familiar picture from a memory
I've yet to make.
Me, too in awe to put it all together,
and her,
too wise to tell me the picture is never the point.
Some things are meant to be learned, not taught.
She laughed, and even the wind stood still
in admiration.

subway stops and puzzle pieces

To end a love, before its time, is to rip two worlds asunder

With every atom, the universe screams out, its cries a piercing thunder.

To look into a lover's eyes, and know your gaze shall not meet tomorrow

A crushing curse, a bleak despair, to fall prey to such a wretched sorrow!

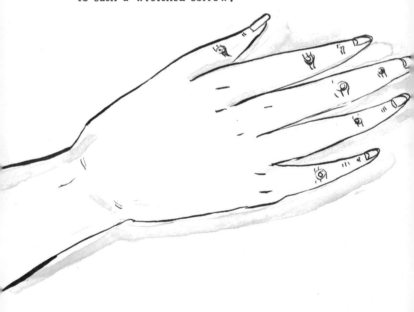

The cold betrayal of one's own heart can rip
a soul atwain

Sliced through and through with the bitter
knowledge that it shall never be the same.

So I beg of you, anyone in love, to protect your
lover's heart

For in this world, there's no greater loss than
density pulled apart.

dark materials

I never wrote her poems,
she tore them from me.
Without permission, and
without guilt,
no apology expected.
I never wrote her poems,
she took them from me by
force,
smashing my love onto her
canvas of choice,
my wounds dripping with ink.
I never wrote her poems,
she stole them,
and that, I think,
is what made them all so
beautiful.

They were hers.

                              violated

"Why?" she sobbed, speaking more to the world than she was to me. "Why do we even try to fall in love when getting it wrong is so ugly?"

Only after a full minute of gazing at her tear-lined face was I able to finally whisper, "Because there's so much beauty in getting it right that you'll forget what wrong ever was."

to the one who makes it all worth it

I had to learn poetry in the basement of a
10-story brick building with no windows and
whitewashed walls,
where the most inspiring thing was the graffiti
carved into the bathroom stalls.
Oh, but the business building was new and
quite pristine.
Fresh paint, new desks, and latest hi-def
screens.

Because who cares about art? It's advertising
that pays the bills.
Maybe that's why I write more ads than poems now,
no matter how many of my dreams it kills.

                                        whitewashed

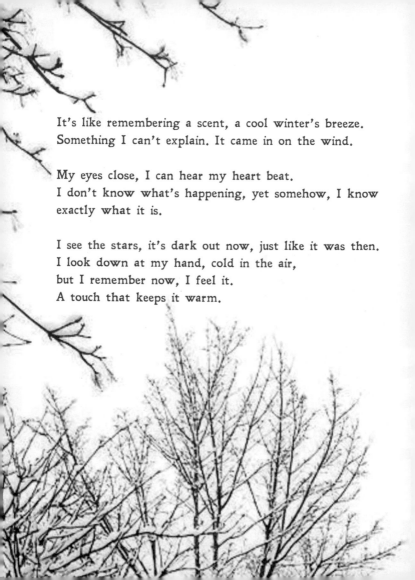

It's like remembering a scent, a cool winter's breeze.
Something I can't explain. It came in on the wind.

My eyes close, I can hear my heart beat.
I don't know what's happening, yet somehow, I know
exactly what it is.

I see the stars, it's dark out now, just like it was then.
I look down at my hand, cold in the air,
but I remember now, I feel it.
A touch that keeps it warm.

I'm walking now, it's like it used to be.
My hand in yours, as you walk next to me.

It smells of leaves, and it smells of snow.
It's that magic time between fall and winter
and I swear I can hear your voice.

The wind blows, and my eyes open
The scent disappears as my hand grows cold.
It must have come in on the wind.
It was just the wind.

just the wind

It wasn't until I saw
constellations in your eyes,
and tears upon your face,
That I finally understood
what it meant
To have the world crash

d

o

w

n

around
you.

We were broken, you and I, in all the right places.

Not in the way so many people romanticize,
with my peaks fitting flawlessly into your valleys,
and your hands perfectly covering my scars.

No.

My mountains hit your mountains,
and my deserts drained your lakes.

My arm fell asleep under you while you slept,
and your hair fell in my face.

We were so imperfectly matched,
so terribly unaligned,
that we just continued to
fall into each other,
until we were such a
tangled mess that I knew
nothing in this world
could ever pull us
apart.

        knotted

My version of God is a 52-year-old man playing
violin in the subway with the case closed,
because it's not about the money, it's all about
the art. She's a heartbroken teenage girl that
grew up to love her kids more than her mother
ever loved her, because I find more
Divinity in Humanity than I have ever
found humanity in God. And don't
call me an atheist, because I
believe in mankind, and my belief
that heaven isn't real only
makes me want to build it here
on Earth. They say that when
you get lost, the best thing
to do is stay put and wait
for help to arrive, but
when you start counting
time in Millennia I
think that rule no
longer applies ...

humanity is a church

The right person, the wrong time.
The right script, the wrong line.
The right poem, the wrong rhyme,
and a piece of you
that was never mine.

timing

While I know correlation is not causality
in today's world of efficiency,
I find beauty the most common casualty.

concrete nightmares

You can be afraid of
lightning, or you can go
dancing in the rain,
and if you look at love
hard enough, you'll find
it's quite the same.

fearless

I believe in alternate realities,
and why shouldn't I?

Because while we couldn't make it work,
we must exist somewhere.

Sure, we made mistakes,
but we must have figured it out.

Somewhere.

Somehow.

I have to believe in other worlds,
because if there isn't at least one universe
where you and I exist,
together,
then how am I supposed to believe that anything
is real?

somewhere

It's you. Every single time it's you.
I want to hold your head in my
hands as my lips brush against the
softness of your skin and I know
you don't need me, but you want
me and I want you back and there's
nothing in this world that will
stop me from choosing you every
night before I fall asleep and every
morning when I wake up because
there's magic to the choice, and I
promise that every single time I'll
choose you. Always you.

a run-on sentence

I aspire to be more like the *leaves*.

To live with such *purpose*,

to have such *beauty in death*.

aspirations

Without the "happily," "ever after"
seems more like a prison sentence,
so excuse me while I take my time
to get it right.

28 and counting

I don't write poems.
I sacrifice myself
to the storm,
and the rain
writes all my pieces.

vessel

I'm **proud** of being broken
Only those brave enough to take
something apart will ever understand
how the pieces go together.

perspective

"What are you thinking about?" she asked, a playful smile dancing across her face.

"Just thinking about how you were worth the wait."

"Oh yeah, what was worth the wait?" she asked as she moved closer, biting her lip the way I liked as her happiness flirted effortlessly with mine.

Now, I knew she was trying to be sexy, but I stopped to consider the question. I know she was looking for something poetic and beautiful, and she deserved it, but only one simple answer came to mind, no matter how hard I tried. Poetic only in its simplicity, beautiful only in its truth. So, with a calmness that betrayed my racing heart, I whispered,
"What wasn't?"

revelation

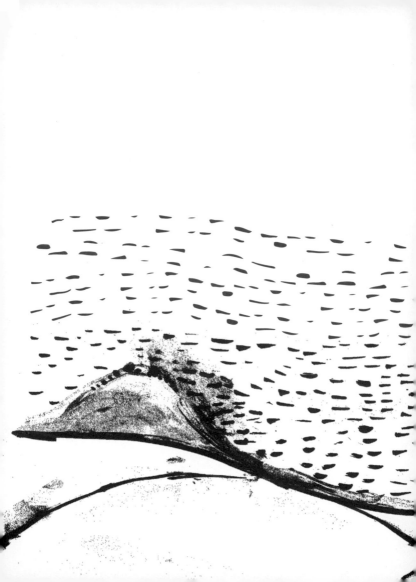

Rainwater and riptides.
Mountaintops and countrysides.
Hurricanes and island breezes.

her

There is magic in every mind that
allows it.
For some, it washes over us like
tidal waves,
drowning us in its power.

But for others, it exists only in the
minds of children,
their own view of the world as dry of
magic as the Sahara is of water.

So while I judge no human,
I pity those who count themselves
amongst the latter.

if only they could see

"Maybe, one day, after all the dust
has settled, you'll find it in your heart
to love me again."

And maybe, after you've grown and
can look back on all this with a
stronger heart and clearer mind,
you'll realize how foolish it was
to think I would have ever stopped
at all.

                                always

I think the classics have ruined us.

"Oh, my love, I see nothing but stars inside your eyes,
I am but dirt, and you, my darling, a beautiful sunrise."

Bleh.

I'm over it.

Not because those moments and feelings don't exist,
but because they take away from the ones that matter.

Like how every time we go out,
we steal a candle from the bar.

My favorite memories of you aren't on mountaintops,
they're in elevators and subway stops.

In hidden rooms in haunted mansions.

I've fallen more in love with you in the dark corner
of speakeasies
than I have in any garden,
and the sunrise means nothing

when my favorite day with you started with us
waking up at noon,
last night's clothes shed hungrily across the floor.

This is how we fell in love.

These are our modern fairytales.

modern fairytales

Photography credits

Pages 64–65 © Ken Towne

Page 66 © Simon Jackson, follow him on Instagram @indys_shots

Page 69 © CICO Books / *ph* Rick Haylor

Page 73 © Antony de Rienzo, follow him on Instagram @antonyderienzo

Page 74 © Anne Johnson, follow her on Instagram @anniemay_1

Page 75 © Clare Sanford, follow her on Instagram @claresanford

Pages 76–77 © Anne Johnson, follow her on Instagram @anniemay_1

Page 78 Shutterstock / © ker_vii

Pages 84–85 © Ryland Peters and Small / *ph* Paul Massey

Page 87 © Ryland Peters and Small / *ph* Debi Treloar

Page 89 © Ryland Peters and Small / *ph* Clare Winfield

Page 91 iStock / © zodebala

Page 94 © Ryland Peters and Small / *ph* Debi Treloar

Page 95 © CICO Books / *ph* Holly Joliffe

Pages 96–97 Shutterstock / © Carlo Fornitano

Page 100 © CICO Books / *ph* Simon Brown

Page 101 © Ryland Peters and Small / *ph* Peter Cassidy

Page 102 © Ryland Peters and Small / *ph* Rachel Whiting / The home of Desiree of VosgesParis.com in Amsterdam

Pages 104–105 © CICO Books / *ph* Kim Lightbody

Page 108–109 Shutterstock / © Denis Belitsky

Page 110 © Anne Johnson, follow her on Instagram @anniemay_1

Page 113 © Ryland Peters and Small / *ph* Rachel Whiting / Joy Cho—designer and blogger of Oh Joy

Page 117 Shutterstock / © KC Jan

Pages 120–121 © Tia Lovisa, follow her on Instagram @tltraveler

Page 123 © Ryland Peters and Small / *ph* Paul Massey

Page 125 © CICO Books / *ph* Richard Boll

Page 126 © Simon Jackson, follow him on Instagram @indys_shots

Page 129 © Ryland Peters and Small / *ph* Clare Winfield

Page 131 Shutterstock / © OZMedia

Page 134 Shutterstock / © photoBeard

Page 139 © Ryland Peters and Small / *ph* Clare Winfield

Pages 140–141 © CICO Books / *ph* Richard Boll

Acknowledgments

To all the people who inspired me to write
a poem about them, please know that this
book is yours as much as it is mine.

To my family and friends. Not every poem
is written in the light, and your support
through the darkness is the only reason any
of these pages exist.

To Carmel, Cindy, Eliana, and the rest of
my team at CICO Books for their tireless
effort and casual definition of "due date."

And, lastly, to all my readers, you have
no idea what you mean to me. If you
have made it this far, truly, and from
the bottom of my heart, thank you.
For everything.

K. Towne Jr. is a poet and dreamer whose love- and whiskey-inspired poems have gained him online fame. His work has been featured by a wide variety of online publications, including *LifeHack*, *QuoteCatalog*, and *Teen Vogue*, and in 2017 he was named "Instagram's most romantic poet" by *YourTango*. Find him on Instagram: @k.towne.jr. He currently lives and works in Brooklyn, New York.